How to Relieve Stress

Stress Management Techniques For College Students

Roxanne Richards

How to Relieve Stress: Stress Management Techniques For College Students

ISBN: 978-0692865811

Legal information and disclaimer:

The purchaser of this publication assumes full responsibility for the use of these materials and information.

Published by: Roxanne Richards

Content⏎

	Pages

Dedication

I dedicate this book to my students, those I have come in direct contact with in the classroom or in my counselling sessions. To the students whom I have never met, I hope this will be a useful resource for all of you.

I also dedicate this book to my parents, Yvette and Cecil Richards, whose commitment to helping those in need have influenced my career as a mental health professional.

Introduction

I've always been moved with compassion when working with students who are overwhelmed by their circumstances and are so crippled by them that even searching for help becomes an extremely difficult task. In life, we often need someone or something to help push or cushion us. May this guide be either a push or cushion to help you to the next stage of experiencing good mental health.

Chapter 1: What Is Stress?

Stress is a state we experience when there is a discrepancy between perceived demands and our perceived ability to cope. It is the body's adaptive response to changes in the environment in which it exists. Some stress is healthy and is known as "eustress", which is a term coined in the 1970's, by Hans Seyle. Stress that is intense or prolonged can be unhealthy and cause physical harm, which Seyle described as distress. College students often experience a high level of stress resulting from their efforts to meet the demands of a busy academic schedule coupled with other life challenges. When stress is normal and healthy, it acts as a positive outlet that helps to accomplish goals. It's the motivation you feel, for example, when working on a challenging assignment for a course that is important for your major. When stress is negative, it can be distressful, mainly leading to poor health and other negative outcomes. If not handled well, stress can be both physically and psychologically crippling, which can result in many symptoms, including:

1. headaches;
2. cramps;
3. tension in the back, neck and forehead;
4. body aches;
5. increased physical symptoms of anxiety and depression;
6. sleep pattern changes;
7. fatigue; and
8. digestive problems.

Stress triggers psychological problems including:

1. anxiety,

2. depression,

3. memory lapses,

4. confusion, and

5. lack of concentration.

It is normal for human beings to experience some form of stress; however, it is critical that stress is managed well. In order to effectively address this problem, it is important to examine the reasons or cause of stress and how to use effective coping skills. This guide will help college students and other individuals who want to regulate stress well.

Chapter 2: How Stress Works

What are some of the main stressors in your life? It is important to note that each individual deals with stress differently. Stress can be viewed on a spectrum from minor to highly intense. Stress response enables humans to handle life challenges. A prime example is being motivated to work harder after getting an unexpected low grade on a term paper. I find, from years of experience and through direct observation of others, that stress appears to have the ability to paralyze both the mind and body.

The body has a special way of handling danger, which is called the "fight or flight" response. This occurs when there is an impending threat and individuals respond by choosing to either fight or flee. Likewise, the body's response to stress is that it prepares for fight or flight through a physiological response. The cerebral cortex will send a message to the hypothalamus, which stimulates the sympathetic nervous system. This results in an increased heart rate, muscle tension, changes in the breathing rate, and secretion of corticoids by the adrenal gland. This increase in heart rate also affects digestion and leads to the overall breakdown in the immune system, making an individual susceptible to illnesses.

Activation of this response will occur by a threat that is real or imagined. A real threat can be a failure of an exam, death of a loved one or getting into a physical altercation with a family member. A threat may also be imagined, such as having thoughts of exam failure with no evidence to support the idea. Stress for other students could also be a result of feeling very lonely and confused while transitioning to a college campus from another state or country. Another stress inducer could be having to adjust to a completely different culture or way of life, through language, food, or social interactions. An individual could also become stressed just from the thought of not being liked by persons in a new surrounding or culture. For some, it can be very stressful not fitting into the crowd, enjoying one's major, struggling with mental or physical health concerns, family conflicts, not being understood by anyone and so much more. Students who have children, are trying to find their purpose, as well as those going through family transitions, including a divorce or being abandoned by a loved one, cannot be overlooked. When the threat or stressful event has passed, then the body usually returns to its normal state.

Daily hassles are regularly occurring conditions and experiences that can threaten or harm our well-being. If these regular conditions accumulate, they can lead to chronic stress. Therefore, it is important for college students to constantly manage ongoing stressors. Having the stress response constantly activated can lead not only to an increased risk for diseases but mental breakdowns as well.

Chapter 3: Stress Management Techniques

Perceived Ability to Cope

Your college campus usually offers counseling services that provide mental health support. Once you find that you are experiencing symptoms related to stress and you are feeling incapable of re-adjusting, set up an appointment with your counseling center and get professional support to work through the stressors. One way to start managing stress is to examine your thoughts and perceptions. Sometimes there is a recurring irrational thought that is causing you to feel stressed that may need to be examined. Some mental health practitioners may address this through the use of Cognitive Behavioral Therapy, which is identifying and disputing or restructuring thoughts that are provoking. This process will help to alleviate anxiety and stress.

We all experience stress in different ways depending upon our personality, our exposure and our resilience. When we perceive we have the ability to deal with a stressful situation successfully, a feeling of success and achievement can be gained. Maintaining balance between good stress to motivate us and encourage us to grow and our ability to cope with the stress is possibly the key to remaining healthy.

Examine Your Thoughts

Identify thoughts that you have as a student that may trigger feelings of being overwhelmed and unable to cope. A lingering thought could be, "I don't belong here like the other students in my class." Dispute this thought with evidence: What proof do you have for this thought? Tell yourself that you would not be in college if you did not have grades and intellectual capacity the ability to begin with. Sometimes the thought will continue to linger but you have to ensure that you keep disputing and depowering the thought by allowing yourself to think about it, rather than avoid it. Examine each thought and ask yourself whether those thoughts are reasonable or are you being irrational in your thinking. Try to dispute each thought with evidence to support the idea.

Another thought could be, "I am a failure and won't make it through the semester." Tell yourself that, although you have challenges, you can still remain focused and succeed.

Also, tell yourself also that, with proper preparation, you can make it through if you don't give up. Your perception that you can cope or overcome a situation, even if the circumstances appear impossible, can be effective. Having that perception can help to alleviate the effect of a negative thought.

There are also few self-talks that may be used to encourage yourself. Coaching yourself where you constantly use self-talks may be applied to a stressful event. For instance, a reoccurring fear of a professor yelling at you in front of a class:

1. Say to yourself, "No this is not true."
2. Take a deep breath, count backwards from 10 to 0.
3. If I do this, then this will not happen.
4. Then focus.
5. Stay focused.

Affirmation of Self

As students, you may often feel discouraged when not affirmed by others. Sometimes, authority figures or even your peers will unintentionally belittle you. For some, it can be hearing a professional, family member or friend imply that you are not capable in a particular field of study. This can crush your dreams and make you want to give up, but affirming your self is a key way of staying focused and encouraged enough to pursue your dreams.

1. Engage in conversations with persons who initially motivated you to make this career decision.
2. Keep abreast of current information in your field of interest that is inspirational.
3. Engage in self-talks that encourage yourself such as, "I can and will do this anyway."

Integrating Positive Activities

Integrating positive activities is a good approach to confronting and managing stress. Spending quality time with family and friends is a good way to relieve negative thoughts and emotions.

It is highly recommended that you have someone who you can call on to vent when having a bad day. Getting involved in clubs and social groups when there is no circle of friends is a good start. For students who have friends and family (i.e., a uteam of loved ones who will be able to encourage you), those individuals are reliable sources of support. Your friends don't need to be physically present to support you. For instance, you may have a friend one million miles away who is very supportive and has influenced you positively. You can maintain that connection by Skyping, Facetiming, or some other means. The support you have with that friend will help you to relieve and manage stress. Sometimes, things may feel a lot more stressful when family is far away but keeping connected to them is important.

For many students, making friends in college is a challenge. Participating in various clubs and activities that are available on your campus is a good way to find and make friends. Make a conscious effort to go and greet someone and introduce yourself and become a part of a larger network. Commuting students would have to research what groups of interests are held at convenient times in which they can become involved. Students who are from another country and find that they have stress related to communicating and meeting people in a new culture may want to connect through their college/university's international affairs office. Usually these offices have resources that are helpful including social events planned specifically to meet the needs of these students.

Do not be discouraged if you are trying to meet and connect and it feels as if it's not working out. Finding the right fit of friends and activities usually takes time. However, consistent effort is very important. Always seek professional help in your counseling center if you feel that your efforts are still unsuccessful.

Exercise

Exercise is a key strategy to managing stress. I would highly recommend that college students make this a part of their weekly schedules. Exercise produces endorphins, "the brain's natural pain killer", which enable a positive feeling and interact with the brain to change the perception of pain. That kind of energy is needed to survive a busy schedule. For instance, a student with a heavy course requirement and dealing with family conflicts, as well as struggling with symptoms of depression, would benefit.

It is good to get out and go to the gym at least three times for the week. The energy and confidence you will gain though exercise might be a challenge to start but will certainly give you a sense of accomplishment and motivation to keep working towards your dreams. This applies to all students in all areas of specialization. Make use of your campus gym and try not to think that walking unintentionally around campus for classes is enough exercise.

You need to make a conscious effort to schedule a structured time to work out. You can get involved in dance, swimming, tennis or some other physical activities that you love, and most college campuses may have these resources. You may improvise by engaging in a work out video or off campus activities. Any consistent involvement in sports that enables a physical work out keeps the stress levels down.

Eating Behaviors

When stressed, it is likely that we will want to eat high calorie foods, usually with high sugar content, and foods that make you feel good temporarily. However, it is very important to maintain a balanced diet with the right nutrients to give you adequate energy needed to make it through a challenging semester. Eating unhealthy, especially when highly stressed, will increase your chances of health problems, including diabetes and hypertension. Students may find it more convenient to grab junk food rather than taking the time to prepare a meal. In the long run, this practice really does not pay off. In fact, it is costly both financially and health wise. A good solution is to designate a day on the weekend when you can prepare meals for the following week. Drink loads of water throughout your day and factor in your fruits and vegetables. Students who live in dorms can easily support each other when possible. You will find that you will have the kind of motivation needed when supported by others. If you need further support and have a serious concern getting energy needed, visit your physician or your health center.

The American Student Health Access Survey (2014), in its report of college students who have been diagnosed or treated by a professional within a 12-month period, revealed a wide range of illnesses experienced by students. Although many illnesses may go unreported, there is no doubt that a high percentage of students are at risk for poor health. Health is paramount to the experience of college education. Therefore, it is important that you manage stress so that it will not exacerbate health problems.

54.8 % of college students (44.7% male, 61.2% female) reported being diagnosed or treated by a professional with one or more of the following conditions within the last 12 months.

Physical Activity and Public Health

The American College of Sports Medicine and the American Heart Association (2007) recommends moderate-intensity cardio or aerobic exercise for at least 30 minutes on five or more days per week or vigorous-intensity cardio or aerobic exercise for at least 20 minutes on three or more days per week.

Stop Breathe-Reflect-Choose

The following four-step technique can help persons alleviate stress:

1. Drop everything that you are doing for a few minutes. Once you are less stressed, you are more capable of taking on the challenge of your assignments or preparing for an exam. It's best to stop, regroup and then proceed. So STOP for a few seconds whatever you are doing and cease the ruminative negative thoughts that have been flowing through your mind.

2. BREATHE: Now, take at least 3-5 deep breaths, inhale through your nose and exhale through your mouth.

3. REFLECT: Try to ask yourself rational questions about the way you are feeling and your current situation. Ask the

following questions: Is this a crisis? Is worrying and getting in a panic state helpful? What specific steps can I do to solve this problem? Will this really matter in 2-6 weeks? Look at all aspects of the situation.

4. CHOOSE: Though it may not seem or feel that way, you

can choose to react in a positive way. The power is in your hands to choose to control your reactions in the midst of stress. You don't have to choose the imminent response of irritability, anger, frustration or being upset. Choose to take charge of how you would respond.

In time, practice will help you master the S-B-R-C Technique developed by Dr. Herbert Benson and Ellieen M. Stuart.

Progressive Muscle Relaxation Technique

Consult with your physician if you have a history of muscle spasms or back problems, so that PMR does not exacerbate any pre-existing conditions. Progressive Muscle Relaxation was developed by Edmund Jacobson in 1939 as a suggestion to help with tense muscles. It enables personal awareness of tension and relaxation. Recommended practice for full PMR is twice a day for a week before using the shortened version.

Always practice PMR alone in a quiet environment, with no music, electronics or other distractions. When the steps are repeated, you learn to recognize the feelings associated with tense muscles and completely relaxed muscles. The idea is to tense your muscles for five to seven seconds then relax.

1. Get into a comfortable position that you find to be most relaxing. Start with pointing your toes downward while feeling the tension. Then, point your toes upward, feel the tension in your calves. Start taking deep breaths, inhale, and then exhale and relax.

2. Next, try tightening your buttocks and feel the tension, then your thighs by pressing your heels very hard for 5-7 seconds. Hold the tension, take a deep breath and relax.

3. Now, tighten the stomach muscles by holding in for 5-7 seconds. Exhale and relax.

4. Now, bend your elbows and clench your fist at the same time. Tense the muscles until they feel tight. Then, straighten your arms, shake out your hands, take a deep breath and relax.

5. Now, pull your head in and hunch your shoulders, almost like a turtle. Press your chin in against your chest and make sure to tighten the throat. Allow yourself to feel the sensation for 5-7 seconds, then drop your shoulders and allow your head to fall forward. Slowly roll your head to the side and back of your neck for the right and left side. Take deep breaths and relax your shoulders and neck.

6. Make a frown and cause your forehead to wrinkle. Squeeze and tighten your eyes and allow your nostrils to flair. Clench your jaws hard and make an "o" with your lips as you keep them tight. Hold it tight for a 5-7 seconds then relax and let go.

7. Breath and feel the tension mentally that was released. Let it go. If you still feel tensed in some areas of your body, repeat in those areas.

Make sure to take breaks, especially when you feel yourself becoming overwhelmed with tense muscles.

Humor

Humor may seem ridiculous, but how do you usually feel after watching your favorite comedy or having a good uncontrolled burst of laughter? Laughter is an antidote to stress. Humor or laughter has a good effect on our bodies. It releases endorphins, giving a sense of calm and well-being. Humor is certainly a great tool to manage stress. Therefore, college students and anyone who is seeking healthier well-being should take time out of their busy schedules to laugh. I would always encourage a good half an hour per day, just to start spending some time on you and laugh it right out. Kick back and simply try your best to focus on a comedy or something that makes you laugh. You can also structure this technique around a social group that influences your ability to laugh. Compile your own videos of laughter and watch them to get this strategy in.

Positive Distractions

Positive distraction is another technique that I would highly recommend to students. This is when you are engaged in an activity that can keep your mind away from stressful events. Being a part of a volunteer activity can be a positive distraction. In fact, pouring out into someone else's life can be strengthening. Sometimes, a history of a pattern of negative thinking can be addressed when a student engages in positive distractions.

Time Management

Some students' stress is directly linked to poor time management and poorly structured study habits. Sometimes, the transition from high school, or from home, is far different, thus making adjustment highly frustrating. If poor time management is hindering you from preparing for classes and assignments in a timely manner, make an appointment with your counseling center for further support. Some of the things you will have to do are as follows:

1. Ensure that you fight the odds and be in all classes so that you are not further behind if you have missed classes and have a problem in this area.

2. Set up a work schedule to match your class time.

3. Practice reading before class and start assignments as soon as they are given.

4. You can do an outline at the end of the day on what you need to accomplish. Once you start doing this, you will find yourself feeling less anxious and worried. Usually, students who are not attempting to work but rather avoid due to fear may wind up feeling more perplexed. Try to set up a daily schedule and find a study partner or group to discuss assignments to review on a monthly basis. This will help you feel that you are sharing the burden. However, if this person or group is not progressing or that your involvement is wasting your time, you may have to leave. Some individuals work well in groups while others find

working alone more beneficial. Test and see what works for you and stick to it.

5. Try starting a "homework night." For example, set aside every other Friday, starting at 9 p.m. or a time that's convenient to you, to complete assignments.

6. Find a study partner who is focused and invite that individual to study with you as soon as the semester begins.

7. Avoid electronics and anything that distracts. Be prepared with the resources needed to complete the assignments.

8. Let your study partner know what you intend to work on for the night.

Sleep

The negative effects of stress can be addressed by a healthy sleeping pattern. Everyone's individual sleep needs vary. In general, most healthy adults are built for 16 hours of wakefulness and need an average of eight hours of sleep a night.

However, some individuals are able to function without feeling sleepy or drowsy after as little as six hours of sleep. Others can't perform at their peak unless they've slept 10 hours. Contrary to a common myth, the need for sleep doesn't decline with age. However, the ability to sleep for six to eight hours at one time may be reduced (Dongen & Dinges, 2000). In college, it may seem almost impossible to sleep for six hours, especially with a hectic college load and for those students who also have to work. How can one possibly sleep? It is important that you put in the work but get in at least six hours of sleep per night. Ensuring that you get structured time to study and work on assignments also makes it more probable to get a good night's sleep. Without rest, you may become irritable and unable to function. Though you may often feel overwhelmed with the assignments and deadlines, you must rest. Getting in your sleep and being in a better mental state will give you the energy required to accomplish these tasks. If you have sleep difficulties, then try working on improving your sleep hygiene (i.e., take a warm bath, do a breathing exercise, get relaxed, dance, think positive thoughts before you sleep).

Ensure you have proper sleep hygiene:

1. Try to eliminate napping throughout the day; it will interfere with your sleep wake cycle;

2. Avoid heavy meals, including caffeinated drinks at bedtime;

3. Stay away from disturbing, emotionally disruptive conversations or movies or anything that will cause unpleasant lingering thoughts and feelings; and

4. Make sure that your bed is comfortable and reserved for sleeping only, as well as avoid studying and doing other activities in your bed.

Chapter 5: Stress Nuggets

1. What is causing this stress in my life?

   Identify possible stressors, take deep breaths and think through each one, telling yourself, "Calm down, calm down."

2. Is this something that can be resolved?

   Take a deep breath and think it through. Can it be resolved at all? Then, say to yourself, "I will take it a step at a time to work it out." If not and it cannot be worked out, you say to yourself, "Let it goooo, Let it gooo...."

3. Break it down and confront the stressors. Make the call or whatever the action you have to take, and address it head on. Taking action could be speaking to your professor and talking about your missed class and assignments.

Prayer

Exercise faith, pray and release the tension of fear, doubt, stress that overwhelms you. Some persons may even decide to do this in a group session.

Dear Lord,

I release my problems about (say them out) my assignments, my family difficulty, etc. I believe that you will fix the impossible in my life or work it out for my own good. With you, nothing is impossible. Give me the strength to fulfil my purpose.

Relaxation Imagery

Whether you are on the train commuting from a hectic day at school or you are in your dorm absolutely frustrated about your academic progress, you can distract your thoughts with relaxation imagery. This is another well-used technique that can help you mentally tap out of a stressful environment and relax yourself in such a way that, when you are confronted with the same challenges, they feel less threatening.

You want to be in a place and time that you feel safe and secured and at peace. Once in a quiet area, with no distractions, close your eyes, imagine you are in the park walking, imagine any time or place where you feel safe. The sun is shining and you love the fresh green trees that are lined to your left and right. You can hear the brook tinkling nearby. Imagine going to the beach where you would watch and enjoy the waves that go and come. Think of your own relaxation, going to a place you love to relax. It could be your home, in your own bed, smelling your mothers cooking. It could be spending time with your childhood friend going to your favorite place. Wherever it is, close your eyes and visualize that scene of total peace and relaxation and take deep breaths. Don't worry if it feels odd at first. It takes times and practice to make something new apart of your routine.

Creative Tools

Writing your thoughts is a very powerful outlet for situations that may seem overwhelming. Students can journal their thoughts as often as possible. A nightly routine of logging thoughts about your day is a great tool to adopt. If you enjoy writing poetry, then spend a few minutes per week out of a busy schedule and feel the therapeutic effect of writing. Using art work and creative means that have worked in the past for you can also be effective. There is a broad range of skills that people have that can be relaxing, different talents and creativity can be used to destress.

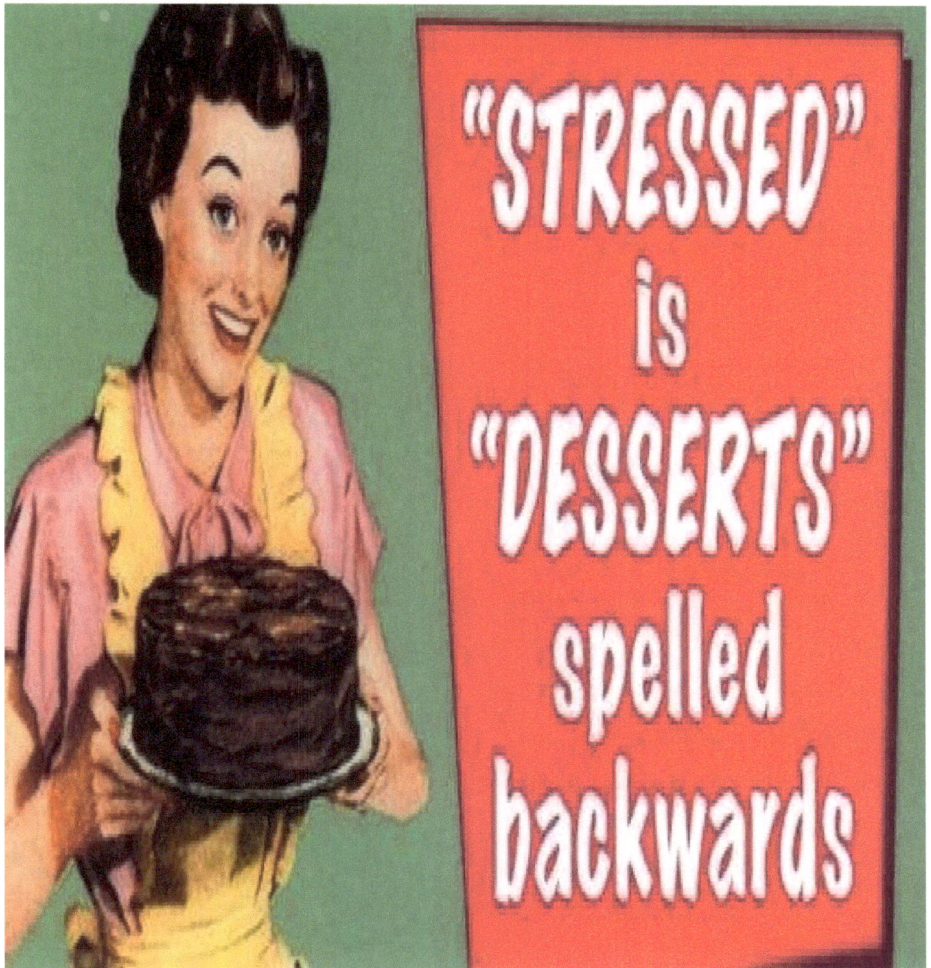

Susan Wilkinson (was Cox)

And all the weight
Started to weigh me down
And it suffocated my happiness
So I took a breath in
And can you feel the rain?
It just started pouring
And it has started to wash it all away
Drenching me in hope
In a joyful downpour
So let it fall
While the world angers
Over smearing makeup
And drenched papers and clothes
Yet I shall be happy
Absolutely joyful with my rain

-Cheyenne Raine

"STRESS!"

I'm pushed not inspired
I'm on a way feeling tired
Got to study all night long
Work so hard or get fired

Sad fact: I had a girlfriend
It's just the pen in my hand
Things revolve in my head
When will all of this end?

Almost forgot what love is
Down on my knees, please
Give me peace, need parties
I'm shut down by this stress

A Cycle

Am I in the right place?
These are the years of decisions
difficulty of transition.
Who am I?
Where am I going?
Working tirelessly but seeing no results,
all seem to want so much but I have nothing to offer.
I can't share my pain
so I hide behind a mask of laughter and pretense.
I want and need you
but fear you will not understand
like all who should.
I cut my pain away
no one cares or knows my sorrows.
I am simply existing,
seems like everything is going wrong
I don't know, I can't do this anymore.
Screaming inside
who will ever know my fears for tomorrow?
Overwhelming thoughts
I don't feel like doing this anymore..
So many assignments,
so much to do and I wasted so much time,
now I cannot face those who invested in me
I am shaking and feel my self-choking,
with attacks of worry and doubt.
The thoughts keep throbbing through my head
I am exhausted with this cycle… but suddenly,
I hear a still soft voice saying "there is hope".
--Roxanne Richards

APPENDIX

How vulnerable are you to stress?

In the space below, answer the following questions by marking 0 (always) to 4 (never), according to the degree each statement applies to you.

__1. I eat at least one hot, balanced meal per day.

__2. I get 7-8 hours of sleep at least for 4 nights per week.

__3. I receive and give affection regularly.

__4. I smoke less than half a pack of cigarettes a day.

__5. I am at the weight that is appropriate to my age.

__6. I have someone within 50 miles on whom I can rely.

__7. I have less than five alcoholic beverages each week.

__8. My income meets basic expenses.

__9. I attend social events and clubs regularly.

__10. I gain strength from my religious belief.

__11. I have a network of acquaintances and friends.

__12. I can find one or more friends to confide in.

__13. I exercise to the extent of perspiration.

__14. I am in good health, which includes my vision, teeth, hygiene etc.

__15. When I become worried or angry, I am able to speak openly.

__16. I have conversations on a regular basis with the people I live with about house problems including chores or bills.

__17. I engage in a fun activity for myself at least once a week.

__18. I am capable of organizing my time effectively.

__19. I drink less than three caffeinated drinks per week.

__20. During the day, I take quiet moments/time for myself.

_____ TOTAL

To score, add the total from 1 – 20 then subtract 20. A number over 5 indicates vulnerability to stress. A score between 25-56 indicates moderate vulnerability. A score over 55 indicates severe vulnerability.

Stress Management Action Plan

Plan of Action

1. Identify three stressors that you need to manage or eliminate.

2. Use one or two techniques discussed above that apply to your situation including a daily use of progressive muscle relaxation.

3. Use this plan for two weeks and monitor how you feel.

4. Get a support partner or friend if possible and express how you are progressing.

Progressive Muscle Relaxation

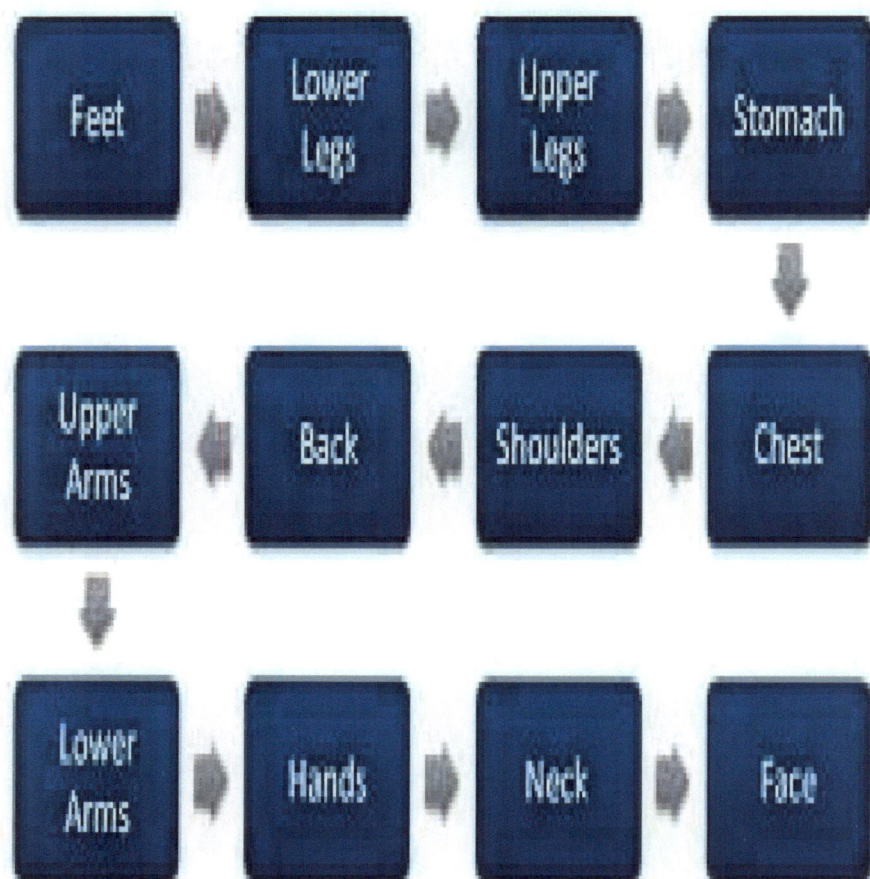

Feet → Lower Legs → Upper Legs → Stomach

↓

Upper Arms ← Back ← Shoulders ← Chest

↓

Lower Arms → Hands → Neck → Face

Resources

Baron, R. A. (1997). *Psychology* (4th ed.). Allyn & Bacon.

Coon, D., & Mitterer, J. O. (2007). *Introduction to Psychology: Gateway to Mind and Behavior* (11th ed.). Belmont, CA.: Wadsworth Publishing.

McKay, M., & Rogers, P. D. (2000). *The Anger Control Workbook.* Oakland, CA: New Harbinger Publications.

Morris, C. G., & Maisto, A. A. (2006). *Understanding Psychology* (7th ed.). Boston Pearson Education Inc.

Rathus, S. A. (2008). *Psychology: Concepts and Connections* (9th ed.). New York, NY: Wadsworth Publishing.

Ryan-Wenger, N., Sharrer, V. W., & Campbell, K. K. (2005). Changes in children's stressors over the past 30 years. *Pediatric Nursing, 31*(4), 282-8, 291.

http://www.forums.familyfriendpoems.com

Van Dongen, H. P. A., & Dinges, D. F. (2000). *Principles & Practice of Sleep Medicine.* Saunders Publishing.

Wade, C., & Tavris, C. (2008). *Invitation to Psychology* (4th ed.). Upper Saddle River, NJ: Pearson/Prentice Hall.

www.ingramcontent.com/pod-product-compliance
Lightning Source LLC
Chambersburg PA
CBHW041223270326
41933CB00001B/26